Binding Up The Broken Hearted

By

Jack Buskey

Binding Up The Broken Hearted
Copyright © 2004 Jack Buskey

All Rights Reserved

ISBN: 1-59352-094-8

3281 Heritage Lakes Blvd.
North Fort Myers, FL
33917
239-543-8211

Published by:
Christian Services Network
1975 Janich Ranch Ct.
El Cajon, CA 92019
Toll Free: 1-866-484-6184

No part of this publication may be reproduced, stored in a retrieval system, or transmitted in any way by any means - electronic, mechanical, photocopy, recording, or otherwise, without the prior permission of the copyright holder, except as provided by USA copyright law.

Printed in the United States of America.

About The Author

Dr. Buskey's parents were devoted to their family, but they were without any knowledge of a meaningful relationship to Christ or His Church.

During High School, Dr. Buskey had a gnawing hunger to know God, but his search was fruitless. At his High School Baccalaureate service he felt the urge to become a minister, but his feelings seemed senseless. It was during his first year of college at the State University of New York, through the ministry and witness of Inter Varsity Christian Fellowship that Dr. Buskey met Christ. It was then he realized the reality of Christ's presence, and the meaning of the call into the ministry.

He transferred to Asbury College, receiving a Bachelor of Arts Degree in 1955. He received a Masters of Divinity Degree from Asbury Theological Seminary in 1957. In 1978 he completed a Doctor of Ministry degree at Drew University School of Theology.

Dr. Buskey filled a student pastorate from 1954?1957 and pastored full time in the Syracuse, New York area from 1957–1987. His pastoral experience included rural churches and suburban churches with a full?time multiple staff. He also pioneered a church which began with three families.

He has taught pastoral counseling, homiletics, church administration, hermeneutics, and survey of church history at Pinecrest Bible Training Center. He taught pastoral counseling at Elim Bible Institute, and survey of Christian Theology in Lee College's extension program.

For several years he directed a counseling center related to Covenant Community Ministries, Fort Myers, Florida.

He founded a two year Biblical Institute in Izhevsk, Russia. Izhevsk is located 1000 K north east of Moscow. Then he served as professor at large for the Church of God Cleveland TN. In this capacity he taught intensives in the denominational schools in Moscow, Manila, Quito, Buenos Aries and Sao Paulo.

He took the retired relationship in 2002 after 50 years of ministry. Now he is free to travel wherever he is invited to minister.

Currently he is a representative for Pinecrest Bible Training Center, Salisbury Center, New York.

Now he is free to travel wherever he is invited to minister.

He may be reached at:

3281 Heritage Lakes Blvd.
North Fort Myers, FL
33917

Phone 239-543-8211

INTRODUCTION

A merry heart doeth good like a medicine; but a broken spirit drieth the bones.
(Prov. 17:22 KJV)

The spirit of a man will sustain his infirmity; but a wounded spirit who can bear?
(Prov. 18:14 KJV)

These verses in Proverbs reveal that the health of the inner man is essential to a victorious and fruitful life. In fact, the state of the inner man may exert more influence upon a person's life than his physical well being. Proverbs 18:14 states that a man can tolerate infirmity, then asks the question, "*Who can endure a wounded spirit?*"

Many have experienced that being born again may not immediately bring healing from all the effects of a broken heart or a wounded spirit.

When an individual's spirit is wounded, a distorted view of life results. This distortion often leads to a loss of hope and ultimate defeat. There are many people who have been born again by the Spirit of the living Christ who live in defeat due to a wounded spirit or a broken heart.

Nevertheless, Jesus binds broken hearts, heals the wounded spirit, and rebuilds the ancient ruins of our inner life. Praise God there is healing for the inner man.

This work defines the problem and then gives the Biblical, theological and psychological keys for healing and release.

Jesus began His ministry in His home town synagogue by reading the prophet Isaiah,

> *Me Spirit of the Lord is upon Me, because He anointed Me to preach the gospel to the poor. He has sent Me to proclaim release to the captives, and recovery of sight to the blind, to set free those who are downtrodden, to proclaim the favorable year of the Lord.' And He closed the book, and gave it back to the attendant, and sat down; and the eyes of all in the synagogue were fixed upon Him. And He began to say to them, 'Today this Scripture has been fulfilled in your hearing.'*
> (Luke 4:18-21)

The healing of broken hearts and wounded spirits, referred to as inner healing, is an integral part of the Lord's ministry, issuing forth from His very being and nature. If you struggle with a besetting sin or a compulsive behavior that keeps you in defeat, the message of this book can set you free.

Preface

Why another book on the subject of inner healing? There are several reasons:

First, to share the fruits of a ministry which, over the past twenty five years, has helped release many Christians from compulsive behaviors or besetting sins, thereby defeating their walk with the Lord.

Second, to offer sound Biblical, theological and psychological principles for the healing of a wounded spirit. My past experience and research on the subject of inner healing indicates that many times ministry to the wounded is not founded on such a basis.

There are books and pamphlets available, as well as recognized teachers who advocate these harmful practices. This work therefore, is an attempt to share a Biblical, theological, and psychological foundation for the ministry of inner healing, and to set the captive free. Thus, this book is also written to sound a warning of some potentially harmful practices which are being followed today.

I am indebted to my wife for input and for Mrs. Nancy Taylor Warner dean of Pinecrest Bible Training Center for editing the original manuscript.

(Please note: All Scripture quotations are taken from the New American Standard Bible unless otherwise indicated.)

TABLE OF CONTENTS

ABOUT THE AUTHOR iii
INTRODUCTION v
PREFACE vii

CHAPTER ONE 3
 The Need
CHAPTER TWO 11
 Biblical Examples Of Inner Healing
CHAPTER THREE 17
 The Theological Basis For Inner Healing
CHAPTER FOUR 25
 The Ministry Of The Holy Spirit In Inner Healing
CHAPTER FIVE 31
 How Christ Heals The Inner Man; The Healing Of the Subconscious; Binding Up The Broken Hearted; Restoring The Ancient Ruins
CHAPTER SIX 41
 Ministering Inner Healing
CHAPTER SEVEN 55
 Some Case Histories

CHAPTER ONE

The Need

Why is it that an individual, having been born of the Spirit, should experience an inner healing? According to Paul, *"If any man is in Christ, he is a new creature; the old things passed away; behold, new things have come"* (II Cor. 5:17). It would seem then, that each new creation in Christ should experience complete wholeness, for hasn't the old passed away? Does the born-again believer's need for inner healing mean that God's promise is lacking?

Some believers fear that acknowledging their need for inner healing would be a denial of their faith. Thus, they have remained in bondage to unhealthy emotions and compulsive behavior patterns. Many believers struggle with besetting or recurring sins in their lives. They do not understand why they should have to deal with the past if they are truly new creatures in Christ.

The individual with a compulsive behavior pattern motivated by a wounded spirit, is set up for a vicious circle of failure and repentance. Praise God for His unfailing and infinite mercy by which He forgives over and over again; but His desire is to set us free.

There are those who despair that one may slip back into the same sin only so many times. This continual failure has led many to turn away, either because of self-condemnation or because they eventually doubted God's ability to deliver them. Some have lost faith in God altogether.

Let me share an **encouraging word to those who** have not yet been released from these types of bondage. You can be set free, and until you are, God's grace is without limit.

Peter asked Jesus,

Lord, how often shall my brother sin against me and I forgive him? Up to seven times? Jesus replied, I do not say to you, up to seven times, but up to seventy times seven.

(Matt 18:21-22)

Jesus was not limiting forgiveness to a count of 490. "*Seventy times seven*" was a symbolic way of saying infinitely, for who of us would keep such records?

So that you are impressed with God's infinite grace, consider what Jesus taught His disciples. "Be on your guard! If your brother sins, rebuke him; and if he repents, forgive him. And if he sins against you seven times a day, and returns to you seven times, saying, 'I repent,' forgive him." Does Jesus practice what He taught? Of course He does!

To address the question of besetting sin in a born again Christian's life, we need to come to grips with some terms. A besetting sin is some behavior or thought

Chapter One: The Need

pattern that you cannot get victory over regardless of how much you have prayed, how often you have repented, or how hard you have tried. I refer to such besetting sin as a compulsive behavior. It is a behavioral disorder or condition that just will not yield to repentance, prayer, will power, or even exorcism. Some will say that this type of besetting sin is caused by demons which control the person's behavior. On rare occasion this may be so, but the majority of those who have come to me with such compulsive behavior were not being controlled by a demon or a spirit, but were rather the victims of a wounded spirit.

Now why is it this wounded spirit was not healed by the New Birth experience? When Jesus enters your life and you are born of the Spirit, you are "saved." Positionally, you now stand robed in the righteousness of Christ. Because you are forgiven, you are justified. In other words, God sees you as if **you had** never sinned.

If we confess our sins, He is faithful and righteous to forgive us our sins and to cleanse us from all unrighteousness.
(I John 1:9)

Therefore having been justified by faith, we have peace with God through our Lord Jesus Christ, through whom also we have obtained our introduction by faith into this grace in which we stand; and we exult in hope of the glory of God.
(Romans 5:1-2)

Being clothed in His righteousness, and justified by His grace makes us perfect in God's sight; but situationally we are the same person. Being a new creature means we have been given a new desire, a new motive, a new direction and a new purpose for life. We know Him, and because of a personal relationship with Christ our whole purpose for life is new. With this new purpose begins the process of growth into the image of Christ as little by little He changes us.

Now with new life and a whole new purpose we become sensitive to all that is not Christ-like in us. No longer can we excuse our sin as being merely human, nor do we judge ourselves by each other; but now we desire to please Him; we want to be like Him.

If we are honest with ourselves, we will readily admit that even though we are forgiven and positionally justified, the Lord still has much work to do in our lives. How true are the statements, "Be patient with me; God isn't through with me yet," and "Excuse this mess; Christian under construction."

From the time we ask the Lord into our lives He begins to remake us. Paul describes the process like this, "We are to grow up in all aspects into Him, who is the head, even Christ" (Eph. 4:15b). When we are **born** again we are forgiven immediately. Then begins the life long process of growth. Positionally we are perfect before God; situationally we enter the growth process which gradually changes us.

Students of theology will recognize that I have been referring to God's imputed righteousness. That is, without any merit of our own, we have His righteousness, so that when a holy and just God looks at us He does not see us as we are, but through the holiness of Christ. Next the process begins of God imparting righteousness to us, or remaking us so that we actually become righteous. He covers us, then remakes us. One is immediate and complete, the other is a life long growth process that will be completed in eternity.

Chapter One: The Need

There are some things from our past that may hinder this growth process. At least two problem areas are quite often caused by past hurts. One of these areas is that of a phobia. A phobia is an irrational fear. Anyone who has counseled will have met people who are obsessed with an irrational fear. When you try to help these people even the Christian counselee is incapable of responding. Irrational fear will not yield to faith, or being cast out in Jesus name, or to positive confession, exhortation, or counseling.

What is needed is a revelation of the cause of the fear that is forgotten, yet continues to influence the mind. For example, one man had claustrophobia, a fear of closed in places. It was so acute that he could not ride in an elevator, or be in a small room, under a vehicle, or in any kind of crawl space without inner panic. When it was discovered that as a small boy he had been trapped in an elevator, the irrational fear left. The boy had forgotten that terrifying experience of being trapped in an elevator, but that experience had influenced his present emotions.

The irrational fear was not caused by a lack of faith, nor would it yield to exhortations to believe God, trust His Word, make a positive confession, or any other attempted ministry. It did yield to a revelation of the cause of the fear. The cause was not the devil or a demon; it was caused by a wounded spirit through a fearful experience in childhood, and forgotten as an adult.

Another problem area is compulsive behavior. An example would be kleptomania, when a person compulsively steals. Kleptomaniacs do not steal because of need or because something has value, but it is a compulsive behavior. It is not a moral issue. It will not yield to exhortations not to steal or threats of punishment. In fact, a person threatened with capital punishment would still steal. They may even steal something of no value or something they couldn't use or both. They steal because they are driven by a compulsion.

There are many compulsive behavior patterns such as lying, lust, gluttony, and irrational temper tantrums. I am not suggesting that each of these habits is a compulsive behavior. It may simply be habit, lack of discipline, or deliberate decisive immoral behavior.

I am suggesting that when a person is born again and is trapped by a besetting sin that has defeated them over and over again and they have tried everything to be set free, it very well may be a compulsive behavior.

Let me point out that to deal with this problem from a behaviorist approach or with exorcism does a lot of damage. When one attempts to change behavior through giving a faith formula, or by a strong exhortation to repent and live right, or some other way to change the behavior without the underlying cause being healed, the person is doomed to failure, self condemnation, and possibly the condemnation of others. This condemnation leads to self-rejection and often rejection of others.

If exorcism is tried, it will fail because you are not dealing with the devil or demons, but a wounded spirit that needs healing. Attempted exorcism often results in the person suffering from the notion that they may be demon possessed.

So we see that even though a person is born again, they still have to be changed little by little into the image of Christ. We know that some people have emotional problems, behavior patterns, and phobias that do not

MARY UHOH
PINECREST

mica_egoyu@yahoo.com

315.429.8521

Chapter One: The Need

respond to exhortation, faith, or exorcism. These are emotional and behavioral problems which are caused by a wounded spirit. The remedy comes through Jesus healing the wounded spirit.

After over thirty years of pastoral experience and extensive counseling, I have witnessed many people set free from these emotions, behavior patterns, and phobias. Jesus is in the business of healing us and setting us free. The rest of this book is about the **Biblical** basis of God's nature in relation to spiritual healing and how He will heal you.

Chapter Two

Biblical Examples
Of Inner Healing

The question is often asked, "If inner healing is valid, why aren't there examples in the Bible?" There are. They just aren't called inner healing, but a study of the account reveals that what we term "inner healing" actually took place.

One example is when Peter experienced the vision of a sheet being lowered with all kinds of animals and he heard the command to kill and eat.

> *Peter replied, 'By no means, Lord, for I have never eaten anything unholy and unclean.' And again a voice came to him a second time, 'What God has cleansed, no longer consider unholy.*
> (Acts 10:9-29)

Peter didn't understand what the vision meant until the people came from Cornelius requesting Peter to come with them to Cornelius' house and minister.

To understand Peter's need for inner healing, we need

to know that Peter had been taught to despise the Gentiles, especially the Romans. The Romans had occupied Judea and the Jews chafed under their rule. From the time of Peter's childhood he had been prejudiced against Gentiles, particularly Romans.

Peter was being asked to go to a Roman house. In fact, this Roman was an officer in the Roman army. Peter had been taught and believed that to have anything to do with a Gentile would defile him.

We note Peter's struggle by the introduction of his message to those gathered at Cornelius' house.

> *And he said to them, 'You yourselves know how unlawful it is for a man who is a Jew to associate with a foreigner or to visit him; and yet God has shown me that I should not call any man unholy or unclean. That is why I came without even raising any objection when I was sent for.*
> (Acts 10:28-29a)

It is not difficult to read his emotions. He said in effect, if God had not done a number on me, I wouldn't be caught dead in the house with you Gentiles! So much for winning friends and influencing people.

On several occasions Peter had heard Jesus teach that they were to minister to the Gentiles. The problem was that Peter was so prejudiced that he couldn't hear Christ's message. He had been wounded in his spirit to the point where he could not hear Christ's clear teaching and command; and at this point in his life, if he had not been healed, he would not have been able to obey the leading of the Holy Spirit to answer Comelius' call.

For example, when Jesus cleansed the Temple, He said,

Chapter Two: Biblical Examples of Inner Healing

Is it not written, 'My house shall be called a house of prayer for all the nations'–But you have made it a robbers' den.

(Mark 11:17)

Peter heard Jesus quote the Scriptures regarding the Temple as a house of prayer for all the nations.

He also may have heard Jesus teach Nicodemus that,

God so loved the world, that He gave His only begotten Son, that whosoever believes in Him should not perish, but have eternal life.

(John 3:16)

Obviously, "whosoever" includes Gentiles.

After the resurrection and just before the ascension, Jesus gave the great commission,

Go therefore and make disciples of all the nations, baptizing them in the name of the Father and the Son and the Holy Spirit.

(Matt. 28:19)

After the resurrection, Peter had heard Jesus' promise and the commission recorded in Acts 1:8,

But you shall receive power when the Holy Spirit has come upon you; and you shall be My witnesses both in Jerusalem, and in all Judea and Samaria, and even to the remotest part of the earth...

The *"remotest part of the earth"* included the Gentiles.

In addition to Peter hearing these teachings and commands, on the day of Pentecost he preached under the anointing of the Holy Spirit that, 'This is what was spoken of through the prophet Joel:

And it shall be in the last days, God says, that I will pour forth of My Spirit upon all mankind; and your sons and your daughters shall prophesy and your young men shall see visions, and your old men shall dream dreams; even upon My bondslaves, both men and women, I will in those days pour forth of My Spirit and they shall prophesy. And I will grant wonders in the sky above, and signs on the earth beneath, blood, and fire, and vapor of smoke. The sun shall be turned into darkness, and the moon into blood, before the great and glorious day of the Lord shall come. And it shall be, that everyone who calls on the name of the Lord shall be saved.

(Acts 2:17-21)

It is even possible to preach something direct from the Lord under the anointing of the Holy Spirit and not have the truth of the message become part of your own life because of an inner barrier.

So even after Peter heard Jesus teach that the Gospel was intended for all, and he had preached it himself, he still needed to have that prejudice removed before he could answer the call to minister to Cornelius.

In that vision on the house top, Peter experienced inner healing that set him free from his prejudice against the Gentiles and enabled him to minister to Cornelius. Note this inner healing took place after his conversion and Pentecostal experience. I believe we have another example of inner healing with Thomas. Thomas' doubt after the resurrection required an inner healing. Remember when Jesus said he was going back to Bethany to minister to Lazarus, it was Thomas who said, "Let us go, that we may die with Him." The disciples knew that for Jesus and His disciples to appear in

Chapter Two: Biblical Examples of Inner Healing

Bethany was so dangerous, it would mean death; yet Thomas was willing to go with Jesus. Thomas was no coward. He was committed to follow Christ even to death.

After the crucifixion, all of the Apostles were disillusioned, discouraged and confused. When Thomas heard a report of the resurrection, I believe he had been so hurt that he was not willing to be hurt again. He obviously wanted to believe, but once around that mountain was enough.

When Thomas was with the Apostles and Jesus appeared, Jesus didn't scold him for his lack of faith, because the issue was not lack of faith or commitment, but rather Thomas' inability to believe because of the inner hurt caused by his lack of understanding regarding the crucifixion. Jesus addressed the need.

He said to Thomas, 'Reach here your finger, and see My hands; and reach here your hand, and put it into My side; and be not unbelieving, but believing. Thomas was healed immediately and confessed, My Lord and my God!
(John 20:27-28)

As we think about these examples of inner healing recorded in the Bible, let us remember that the Scriptures never intended to give us an account of all that Jesus or the Apostles did. John wrote,

And there are also many other things which Jesus did, which if they were written in detail, I suppose that even the world itself would not contain the books which were written.
(John 21:25)

I expect this is also true of all that the Apostles did and experienced in the early church, for we read nothing in the Book of Acts of the ministry of half the Apostles. They too must have had effective ministries. We do have enough examples of inner healings, however, to form a Biblical basis for such ministry.

Chapter Three

*The Theological Basis
For Inner Healing*

Now let us give our thought to the theological basis for inner healing. By theological basis, I refer to the basis for inner healing that is found in the very nature and attributes of God.

The foundational basis for inner healing is rooted in the very nature of God. God is. God has no past or future. He is. One of the dimensions of eternity is that there is no time. Eternity is. I like to call it the "is ness" of God.

We must have a past or we lose our orientation and identity. This has been illustrated by the emotional upheaval experienced by refugees because their past has been uprooted. People who have amnesia also experience severe emotional disturbance because they have lost their past through the loss of memory.

We need a past, but God neither needs a past nor has one. HE IS. The past, present, and future are all one in God. We can express it but we can't understand it or experience it because it is a dimension that we won't experience until eternity.

God not only has no past but He has no future either, for all is in God; He is. The fact that God has no future gives us an insight into prophecy. Prophecy does not cause something to happen; it is simply a revelation of what is going to happen. Jesus indicated this when He told His disciples, *"And now I have told you before it comes to pass, that when it comes to pass, you may believe"* John 14:29. We need a future or we have no hope; but the past, present, and future is all one in God. This is expressed in the Scriptures in several places and in several ways.

When Moses was sent to Egypt to deliver the children of Israel from slavery he asked God,

> *Behold, I am going to the sons of Israel, and I shall say to them, The God of your fathers has sent me to you. Now they may say to me, What is His name? What shall I say to them? And God said to Moses, I AM WHO I AM; and He said, Thus you shall say to the sons of Israel, I AM has sent me to you.. And God, furthermore, said to Moses, Thus you shall say to the sons of Israel, The Lord, the God of your fathers, the God of Abraham, the God of Isaac, and the God of Jacob has sent me to you. This is My name forever, and this is My memorial-name to all generations.*
> (Exodus 3:13-15)

When God identified himself as the "I AM," He was declaring His eternal nature. I Am has no past or future. I Am had no beginning and has no ending. There is no time reference so there can be no past or future, just the ever-present.

Chapter Three: The Theological Basis For Inner Healing

When the Jews questioned the identity of Jesus, He said, *"Before Abraham was born, I AM"* (John 8:58). In making this statement Jesus was saying that He and the "I AM" who spoke to Moses at the burning bush, were the same person. Jesus was saying, I am the "I AM" who spoke to Moses.

They understood very well that Jesus was declaring His divinity. He was saying, "I am God, I am eternal." That is why *"they picked up stones to throw at Him"* (John 8:59).

Jesus' eternal nature is stated in the prologue of John's Gospel,

In the beginning was the Word, and the Word was with God, and the Word was God. He was in the beginning with God. All things came into being by Him, and apart from Him nothing came into being that has come into being.

(John 1:1-3)

One of the reasons the conception of Christ in Mary was by the Holy Spirit is that Christ is eternal. Although Jesus came in the form of flesh through Mary, at the conception it was not a new person who came into being. It was the eternal Christ.

Another instance that reveals the eternal nature of God is Jesus' response to the Sadducee's question regarding a woman who had been widowed and remarried seven times:

In the resurrection, when they rise again, which one's wife will she be? Jesus replied, but regarding the fact that the dead rise again, have you not read in the book of Moses, in the passage

about the burning bush, how God spoke to him, saying, I am the God of Abraham, and the God of Isaac, and the God of Jacob. He is not the God of the dead, but of the living.

(Mark 12:18-27)

When Jesus quoted, "I am the God of Abraham, and the God of Isaac, and the God of Jacob," He was making it clear that God is, and because God is, those who are His are alive. That is, Abraham, Isaac and Jacob were still alive. They were now in an eternal state. If they were not still in existence as more than historical characters, then God couldn't be their God because He is only the God of the living.

Again, Paul makes reference regarding the rock in the wilderness.

For I do not want you to be unaware, brethren, that our fathers were all under the cloud, and all passed through the sea; and all were baptized into Moses in the cloud and in the sea; and all ate the same spiritual food; and all drank the same spiritual drink, for they were drinking from a spiritual rock which followed them; and the rock was Christ.

(I Cor. 10:1-4)

What a revelation. It looked like a rock, it felt like a rock, but it wasn't a rock. It was Christ. The water they had drunk came from Christ.

Consider Christ's comment, *"Or what man is there among you, when his son shall ask him for a loaf, will give him a stone?"* Matt 7:9. Sometimes God's will looks like a stone, feels like a stone, smells like a stone; but when we are obedient we discover it is bread. Yes, the

Chapter Three: The Theological Basis For Inner Healing

Bread of Life. It is true the enemy may make a stone look like bread, smell like bread, feel like bread; but if we are disobedient and eat it, we will discover it to be a stone. Does that sound like the Garden of Eden?

In the wilderness, the Rock was Christ. This is another illustration of the eternal nature of Christ. He is; He has no past and no future. He is eternal, HE IS.

An understanding of the eternal nature of Jesus is very important. This means that the cross did not become a reality on Calvary 2000 years ago. That is when the cross was revealed.

The cross has always been a reality, because it has always been in the heart of God. Anything that is in the heart of God is as real as it can ever be. Regardless of whether it has yet been revealed in history, it is indeed a reality because it is in God. So the historic event was not when the cross became a reality, but rather when it was revealed.

Therefore, when Abraham believed God, the blood of Christ justified him. He knew nothing of the cross of Christ, but God could apply the blood of Christ through Abraham's faith, because the cross was a reality.

This is expressed in Scripture, *"The Lamb that was slain from the creation of the world"* (Rev. 13:8b). It was not a matter of God creating man perfect, man sinning and then God coming up with plan B. No, God was not caught by surprise when man sinned. "The Lamb was slain from the creation of the world" before man was ever created. The cross is eternal, for it is in the heart of God.

Just as Abraham was redeemed by the Lamb not yet revealed, but a reality, we too are redeemed by the Lamb. Not by a Christ who died for us 2000 years ago, but by a current cross; for God has no past, HE IS. When we received Christ into our lives the blood of the cross that was applied to us was and is current. This truth regarding the eternal nature of Christ is crucial in order to understand the theological basis for inner healing.

We can only live in the now. We cannot live one second before it comes, nor can we live one second after it has passed. So the only way one can go to the past is through memory.

When we review the past through memory and meet Christ there, He is not in the past, but in His eternal nature. In other words, He is there in the present, for HE IS.

We know that the experiences of the past influence our perception of the present. We all see life through the experiences, the baggage of our past. Thus, one who has had a past experience which has wounded his spirit, is bound to have a distorted perception.

Through years of counseling, I have discovered that no one is insane, only perceptions are distorted. For example, suppose you entered a room and extended your hand to greet me. If my perception was distorted to the point that I thought you had a gun and were threatening my life, my behavior would be considered bizarre and even insane if I attacked you. On the other hand, if you really had a gun and were threatening my life and I greeted you with a handshake, that behavior would also be considered bizarre.

I believe that people respond according to their perceptions. Thus, no behavior is strange, only perceptions are distorted. We have the key to another's behavior when we understand their perceptions.

Chapter Three: The Theological Basis For Inner Healing

This means that when a Christian exhibits a compulsive behavior pattern, it may very well mean they are responding to a perception that is distorted by a wounded spirit. This problem will not be solved by exorcism, will power, or attempts to change behavior patterns. It will only respond to a healing of the wounds that are causing the distortion. As stated previously this explains why many Christians battle various behavior pattern problems with little or no success. Yet, praise God, He has made a way to escape through the binding of broken hearts and restoring the ancient ruins, through inner healing.

Again, when I traverse the past through my memory and I meet Christ there, He is not there in the past for He has no past. He is there in the dimension of eternity. In other words, if I meet Christ in the past, although I am there by memory, He is there in reality, in the ever-present. I cannot do anything to change the past and Christ won't change past events. He will, however, minister to me in my memories of the past, healing me so that the cause of my problematic behavior is healed.

Chapter Four

The Ministry Of The Holy Spirit In Inner Healing

One of the primary ministries of the Holy Spirit is to reveal Christ. When Jesus prophesied the coming of the Holy Spirit, He said,

> *When the Helper comes, whom I will send to you from the Father, that is the Spirit of truth, who proceeds from the Father, He will bear witness of Me.*
>
> (John 15:26)

Each expression of God revealed in the Godhead has a specific emphasis in relationship and ministry. These are the Father-Creator, the Son-Redeemer, and the Holy Spirit-Revealer, or witness of Christ. It is the Holy Spirit who makes the presence of Christ a reality in our lives.

The Holy Spirit is the presence of God with us. He convicts us of our sin, and imparts the faith to believe in Christ. When we say we have Christ within, we are testifying that He abides within us through the presence of the Holy Spirit.

Christ dwells within us through the Holy Spirit,

Or do you not know that your body is a temple of the Holy Spirit who is in you, whom you have from God, and that you are not your own?
(I Cor. 6:19)

Jesus said of the Holy Spirit, "*He shall glorify Me; for He shall take of Mine, and shall disclose it to you*" (John 16:14).

He said,

But you shall receive power when the Holy Spirit has come upon you; and you shall be My witnesses both in Jerusalem, and in all Judea and Samaria, and even to the remotest part of the earth.
(Acts 1:8)

The Scriptures clearly declare that the Holy Spirit would bear witness of Him, Christ; in other words, He would reveal Christ.

Paul recognized this truth when he wrote, "*No one can say, 'Jesus is Lord,' except by the Holy Spirit*" (I Cor 12:3b). No one can see Christ apart from the work of the Holy Spirit.

It is important to emphasize the work of the Holy Spirit, because the very essential key point in the ministry of inner healing is that the Holy Spirit reveals Christ. It is also crucial that we differentiate between CHRIST BEING REVEALED BY THE HOLY SPIRIT and OUR PICTURING CHRIST IN OUR OWN IMAGINATION. Although visualization has been used by some as a means of ministering inner healing, I believe this to be extremely dangerous, and should have no place within this ministry.

Chapter Four: The Ministry of The Holy Spirit

Visualization is a method whereby an individual is urged to try to imagine Christ in a particular situation. As they deal with the memory of a bad experience, they are told to visualize Christ in that situation. They take the Christ they know from experience and Scriptures, and through imagination try to place Christ in that situation.

Why is this so dangerous? First, whenever we try to visualize Christ in a particular situation, we have the distortion of our own concepts and ideas. When we construct a Christ from our own mind, we create a Freudian Christ. One of Freud's notions was that God was the construction of man's subconscious. Freud said God was the result of a father image coming out of the subconscious. Of course this is an over simplification of Freud, but he rejected belief in God as an objective being existing outside of man's thought. When we visualize Christ we fall into the trap of concocting a Christ of our own making.

Another danger in visualization is that we will always manipulate what we visualize. The manipulation may not be conscious or intended, but the very distortion of our own understanding will distort the image of both the memory and of the Christ we visualize.

As I have read numerous accounts and heard testimonies of various experiences in visualization, there has also been an attempt to change the actual facts of the experience.

For example, a person may have been traumatized by an abusive parent. Let us say that a child who tried to prevent his mother from being beaten by a drunken father, was beaten also. Even though the memory of this may be distorted because of its impact upon the child, the basic facts were so. That is, the father was beating the mother, and the child was beaten trying to protect the mother.

In visualization, a person is instructed to visualize Christ in that situation. In other words, they are to visualize their father as receiving Christ and **His love**, and therefore behaving in a loving way toward them. But this is not what happened, and to visualize it would distort the facts. Furthermore, if the individual is told to imagine taking Christ to the drunken father, and having Christ put His loving arms around their father in his forgiving mercy, they are building a delusion. Whenever this kind of visualization is used in this manner, the actual facts of the past situation are being manipulated. Christ does not change the facts of the past. He heals us from the hurt of them.

If we try to change the facts of the past, that is deception. Granted, the individual may feel better, even behave better, because some pressure has been relieved due to this exercise, but the person has not been healed. What really happened is that they have been deluded into feeling better. Self-delusion will always have a way of manifesting itself in some other harmful behavior or thought pattern.

Many have rejected inner healing because of these practices, and rightfully so. There is a place for visualization, but not in inner healing. We all need to visualize if we are to be creative. For example, an artist visualizes a painting before he paints; an architect visualizes a structure before designing; a musician visualizes a tune before composing, etc. We are to use our imagination creatively, but that is a long shot from using our imagination to create Christ and His ministry to us.

Chapter Four: The Ministry of The Holy Spirit

More could be said about this whole subject in regard to the popular positive confession theology that is based on visualization rather than a surrender to His sovereign will; but the purpose of this work is to focus upon inner healing as such.

Now that we have looked at the dangers associated with visualization, let us consider the contrast between visualization and revelation. When the Holy Spirit reveals Christ, we receive a true image of God. Jesus told Philip, *"He who has seen Me has seen the Father"* (John 14:9).

Everyone who has been converted, or born again, has had a true vision of their own sinfulness from God's perspective. When the Holy Spirit convicts us of sin there is no rationalization. We receive what John Wesley called "a godly sorrow of sin." Christ came into our lives, not by visualization, but by revelation—a revelation of Christ by the Holy Spirit. The Christ that came to dwell within us was not a Christ of our own construction or idea, but the incarnate Christ of God.

In fact, most of us had a lot of unlearning to do as the real Christ became revealed to us through the Scriptures and experience. As the Holy Spirit illuminates Scripture to us, the process of corrective learning begins.

As we join these two truths, we see that God has no past or future, for He is; and it is the Holy Spirit who reveals Christ. Therefore, even though we relive a past experience in our memory, Christ need not return in memory; He is there is reality, for the past and present are the same in God. He cannot change the events of the past, but He does heal their impact on us.

This leads us to the next chapter on how Christ's presence revealed in a past experience heals us.

Binding Up The Broken Hearted

Chapter Five

*How Christ Heals The Inner Man;
The Healing Of the Subconscious;
Binding Up The Broken Hearted;
Restoring The Ancient Ruins*

Rather than choosing from among the above titles for this chapter, it seemed appropriate to use them all and let you select the one you like best.

Even though it is true that a wounded spirit can cause compulsive behavior and is the cause for some of our problems, it is not true that we are the products of what has happened to us. Nor can we blame others for our behavior.

We have no claim to an unhealthy competitive spirit because of our siblings. Nor may we say that we don't trust people because of being betrayed by parents or that we are unable to express love because of being denied the expression of love at home. Whatever excuse we tend to use for our un-Christ-like behavior is unacceptable.

We are not the way we are because of what anyone

has done. Most psychological thought would regard this to be a radical statement. Let me repeat it even more emphatically, WE ARE NOT THE WAY WE ARE BECAUSE OF WHAT ANYONE HAS DONE TO US, *we are what we are because of our response or reaction to traumatic events in our lives.*

We may have reacted to such an experience when we were too young to be held responsible. Regardless, our reaction to the event causes the wounded spirit.

This is one area where we observe a big difference between ourselves and Christ. Christ did not inherit a sinful nature. He went through many traumatic experiences, but because he was not born with a carnal, self defensive nature, He did not react from a negative self-centered soul as we do. Thus, the experiences did not wound His spirit.

For example, His conception and Mary's pregnancy were traumatic events. Mary did not live in a mobile society. She and her family were well known, even for generations. Remember the penalty for fornication was death by stoning. So Mary was pregnant, but Joseph knew he was not the father. Then the Lord revealed the circumstances to Joseph, but there is no indication Mary's parents were informed. Thus, no one else in the community would have known Mary's secret. Talk about social pressure. Do you think that Mary's parents believed her story about conception by the Holy Spirit? Joseph did not believe it until God spoke to him.

Then there was the tedious trip to Bethlehem right when she was due to deliver. These were not the friendly skies of United Airlines. It was a tiresome trip on donkey–great therapy for a pregnant woman! I'm sure no gynecologist would recommend it. It would be worse than an expectant mother traveling a dirt bike over a rough trail.

Chapter Five: How Christ Heals The Inner Man

As if the trip wasn't bad enough, when they arrived in Bethlehem there was no place to stay. We shouldn't be hard on the poor inn keeper. We have been criticizing him for two millennium. Since Joseph and Mary could not travel as fast as others who were required to make this trip to Bethlehem, the town had obviously been full to overflowing for days. Can you imagine the conditions of any small town in America if all those whose ancestors had been born there had to show up at the same time to register for a census?

The inn keeper should be commended for offering what he had. Most of us would have turned them away saying there was nothing we could do. At least he let them use his stall. Well, at any rate, can you imagine the experience of Joseph and Mary in this situation? Do you think they were super-human people who, in spite of the circumstances, were as calm and collected as if they were at home around a campfire with friends and neighbors enjoying a sociable evening?

Then after the birth, Joseph and Mary had to flee Judea for their lives, so they went to Egypt. Jesus, as a young boy, grew up in Egypt–not the most hospitable place for Jews. Jesus grew up a minority in the midst of prejudice and racism where Jews had no civil rights.

Furthermore, it is evident in the Gospels that His family didn't understand Him.

> *And He came home, and the multitude gathered again, to such an extent that they could not even eat a meal. And when His own people heard of this, they went out to take custody of Him; for they were saying, He has lost His senses.*
> (Mark 3:19-21)

In addition to all these experiences, Jesus was misunderstood by His disciples. They didn't understood His purpose until after Pentecost; He was betrayed by one of his own, and a leading Apostle denied Him three times. He suffered the indignities of an unjust trial, public mockery and the agony of the crucifixion. He had the painful experience of rejection by friends and foes, and finally experienced separation from His Father.

In the midst of this, He never received a wounded spirit. There is no evidence that he ever had a wrong attitude or action. Why? Surely not because He did not have bad experiences that could have wounded His spirit. He did not receive a wounded spirit because He never defended Himself. He had not been corrupted by the Fall, nor did He have a self centered nature. He never needed to defend Himself Because He had not been distorted by original sin, He had complete faith in His Father. This faith kept Him from self defense. He remained untarnished by these experiences because of the way He responded to them.

It is not what people do to us, or what we experience that wounds our spirits; it is how we respond.

The issue in the Garden of Eden was trust in the integrity of God. God said to the First Couple, if you will trust me, that I love you, then don't eat of the Tree of Knowledge of Good and Evil. Man didn't trust God's integrity or love. He believed that God was keeping him from something good, something he needed.

So man took matters into his own hands and partook of that tree. Had he believed in God's integrity he would have been lifted by faith to a state of righteousness. Not believing God, he fell into a state of sinfulness.

The new fallen nature of man meant that he now had

Chapter Five: How Christ Heals The Inner Man

to be a self-centered creature in order to survive. It is this self-centered nature that causes man to build walls to protect himself. All of man's coping and defense mechanisms are set in motion by this self-centered nature. The combining of these mechanisms cause us to build walls that imprison us; and this self-protection wounds our spirits.

This concept is important for us to understand, for it will lead us to repentance of our improper response that is the real cause of our hurt. As long as we blame the experiences and what others have done to us for our attitudes and behavior, we cannot be forgiven or healed.

It is true that we may have responded to negative experiences when we were so young in life that we were not accountable for our reactions, but that will change when we go back to that experience in memory and Christ reveals our response. Then we will see the situation and our response in the light of His revelation and become responsible for our response. At that point we must repent if we are to be forgiven and healed.

When I rehearse an experience through memory, the Holy Spirit will reveal Christ's presence in that situation if I ask. That is one of the ministries of the Holy Spirit, but remember the important distinction between the Holy Spirit revealing Christ and my trying to visualize or imagine Him.

We will deal with the mechanics or the techniques of receiving this ministry in a later chapter. For now, let us deal with how Christ ministers to the inner man. How does he heal us from past hurts and wounds?

We can ask the Holy Spirit to search our hearts, for He knows exactly what experiences wounded our spirits.

With precise accuracy, He will bring to our memory the experiences that need healing.

David prayed,

> *Search me, O God, and know my heart; Try me and know my anxious thoughts; And see if there be any hurtful way in me, And lead me in the everlasting way.*
>
> (Psalm 139:23-24)

He was asking the Holy Spirit to bring to light, to his memory, anything from the subconscious that may have hurt him.

In other terms, he was asking the Holy Spirit to psychoanalyze him. Some who minister inner healing systematically begin with the present and go back year by year to early childhood dealing with every memory that has any pain. However, I do not believe that is necessary.

Think of a backlash in a fishing reel, or any rope that is a tangled mess. At first it looks like a hopeless task to untangle it. As you work on it you will discover two or three key knots. When they are taken care of the rest unravels quickly. I believe our mind is like that. There will be several key experiences that became the seed bed for our hurt and hurtful behavior. When the Holy Spirit reveals those, and the Lord heals them, the rest of our life comes into order.

The next key is to ask the Holy Spirit to REVEAL the presence of Christ. I emphasized the word reveal, to remind you of the difference between a revelation by the Holy Spirit and visualization.

Christ's presence may be revealed by the Holy Spirit in the form of light, an image, or a presence. The reality of

Chapter Five: How Christ Heals The Inner Man

His presence is what is important, not the form. One way of recognizing a revelation is that He is very seldom revealed in a way, or in a place, we would anticipate or expect.

He will be revealed in a specific place, like a location within the situation being remembered. Even though He is omnipresent in all places at the same time, there is a focus of His presence in a particular place. Often I have experienced a focus of His presence in a specific place in a room. For example, there have been times during an altar service when there was an awareness of a special focus of His presence around the people ministering and the people being ministered to. That doesn't mean He is not every place else at the same time. It simply means there is a focus of His presence at a specific spot.

There was a focus of His presence at the parting of the Red Sea, at Mount Sinai, in the Holy of Holies, at Mount Carmel, etc. This does not mean that He was not also omnipresent. So in all our life, whether we are aware of Him or not, whether we know Him or not, there is a focus of His presence in every situation. He is always with us.

When the Holy Spirit reveals Christ's presence in a situation from our past, we will become aware of a specific place where there was a focus of His presence. Remember, although we are there in memory, He is there in reality. For Him that situation is in the eternal present.

As we become aware of His presence we also become aware of His countenance. We become aware of His attitude in the situation, whether He is grieved, sad, angry, understanding, etc. His countenance is communicated to us.

We are able to communicate with Him and to ask Him questions. For example, we can ask Him to show us the situation as He sees it, and as He does this we get a new perspective on the situation. This is very important, for we have responded to our perspective of the event. The younger we were, the more crucial this new perspective becomes, because children have a perspective seen through physical and emotional immaturity.

I remember this big hill we slid down when I was a boy. I went back to that same hill as an adult and was surprised to discover how it had diminished to a slight grade. I had the same experience regarding a big high school auditorium. I had not been back there since graduation from high school and when I visited the school as an adult the big auditorium had shrunk. It only held 300 people, but as a high school student who lived in the country, it seemed huge. When Christ reveals the situation as He sees it, we gain a whole new perspective of the situation.

Then we ask Christ to reveal to us how He sees us and the other people involved in the situation. What an experience it is to see people from His perspective. I believe this is what Paul was referring to when he wrote,

For the love of Christ controls us, having concluded this, that one died for all, therefore all died; and He died for all, that they who live should no longer live for themselves, but for Him who died and rose again on their behalf. <u>Therefore from now on we recognize no man according to the flesh</u>; even though we have known Christ according to the flesh, yet now we know Him thus no longer.

(II Cor. 5:14-16)

Chapter Five: How Christ Heals The Inner Man

The love of Christ controlled Paul because he didn't see men through his own perspective, but through the eyes of Christ. When we see people as Christ sees them, then we will have the same compassion for them that Christ has.

As we communicate with Christ, we can ask Him to reveal to us how he sees the people involved in whatever situation we are remembering. As Christ gives us that revelation, we see these people in an entirely different light. We see their emotions, motivation, and perspective.

As we view the situation and the people from His perspective, it is easier for us to understand how we were hurt and why. It becomes easier for us to ask Christ to forgive the people involved. In asking Him to forgive them we can forgive them also.

We also can see how our reactions of resentment, rebellion, jealousy, anger, or whatever it was, caused our hurt. We become aware that what wounded us was the attitude caused by our reaction. As this becomes evident to us we have the opportunity to repent of that wrong reaction and to ask for His forgiveness.

As strange as it may seem, we need to repent from our reactions. Even though we have been wronged, our wounded spirits are the result of wrong reactions. We do recognize that repentance is always optional. This experience puts us in a place of seeing the issue and the cause of the hurt. We can either turn away from Christ and hold on to the hurt, or we can repent and find release and forgiveness.

The way Christ heals the wounded spirit in a person is by revealing the situation and the people as He sees them. We also see our part in the situation, and how our action or reaction caused the hurt. This leads us to forgive others and to ask Christ to forgive them.

It also leads to our repentance from the wrong attitude and actions which were the cause of our long term hurt. As we repent He gives the assurance of His forgiveness and we are freed from the impact of that hurt.

When we repent from a wrong attitude and have forgiven, and have been forgiven, then the sting and the poison is removed from the experience. We are healed and set free.

The events in the situation have not been changed, but its effects have. The experience is not blotted out from our memory, but the memory no longer has control over our attitudes and behavior. In fact, if the memory had to be blotted out, it would indicate that we had not been healed. When we are healed, we do not need to have the memory removed. It is no longer harmful, nor causes hurt any longer.

Chapter Six

Ministering Inner Healing

The first step in ministering inner healing is to determine the need. I do not accept the notion that everyone needs inner healing, nor do I believe that inner healing cures all behavioral problems. Some may have behavior problems caused by rebellion, others by carnality or yielding to the flesh. In rare instances there could be demon activity.

It does not help if a person thinks you are looking for demons, so in this initial stage I employ a simple test for demon activity. As I talk with the person, unbeknown to them, I am silently worshiping the Lord. Demons will respond to Jesus being worshiped. They are able to hear our worship whether it is out loud or silent. I believe if Jesus is being worshiped and lifted up, demons will respond.

Demons have to respond to the name of Jesus for they cannot stand the sight of His presence. Demons are deceptive and are able to hide from people, but they cannot deceive Christ nor can they hide from Him. Whenever and wherever Jesus is recognized and praised, demons react.

We tend to give demons too much attention. If they are not welcome, they must flee at the Name of Jesus. When a person does not want to be rid of demons there is nothing you can do; and Christ won't force a demon out against a person's will. If demon activity is detected and the individual wants deliverance, simply command the demon to leave in Jesus' name and be done with it. If the person doesn't want to be set free, leave the situation. We are not to play around with demons. Either cast them out in Jesus' name or separate from the person.

On the other hand when a person knows the Lord, and has wrestled with some besetting sin unsuccessfully no matter what they have tried, I then suspect the need for inner healing. The sin, or behavior, may be an attitude, an act, or both. It may be anger, a temper, lust, lying, masturbation, resentment, gluttony, or any number of things. These individuals are convicted of the sin, but fall victim to it over and over again.

After a simple test for demon activity, I ascertain through conversation whether the individual really tried to discipline himself. When these areas are dealt with and satisfied, I am then ready to minister inner healing. It is important that a person not seek inner healing as a quick solution to a habit that would yield to repentance and self discipline.

I might add that in over thirty years of counseling, I can count on both hands the times I have encountered demon activity. I think it is unfortunate that people have labeled attitudes as spirits. For example, anger being called a spirit of anger, or lust being called a spirit of lust gives the impression that there is a spirit acting independently of the person. An attitude is an attitude, not a spirit. We don't get rid of an attitude by casting it out. An attitude needs to be changed.

Chapter Six: Ministering Inner Healing

When I am satisfied that a person can benefit from inner healing, the next step is to thoroughly explain the Biblical and theological basis for inner healing. I then present the concept of recalling past experiences through memory, where the Holy Spirit can reveal the reality of Christ's presence in the situation.

I take time to explain the difference between the Holy Spirit revealing Christ and someone visualizing or imagining Christ. Then I explain the procedure. We will ask the Holy Spirit to take control and bring to their memory anything that He knows needs to be healed.

The risk the individual takes is in trusting the counselor with the secrets of whatever memory comes up. If there has been trauma such as having been mugged or raped or perhaps the victim of an accident, then I let them know that they will be expected to do that which they have avoided ever since the experience. I urge them to deliberately remember the experience. They have been trying to extinguish the memory and now the counselor asks them to remember it and to describe it as well. Emotionally, they will experience it again.

After discussing Biblical, theological, and phychological bases and describing the procedure and the risk, I suggest they pray and think about it and return with their decision at the next appointment. This time to think about it without the pressure of the counselor's presence, is important to them. They have already experienced the strain of explaining their problem, and they have learned the inner healing basis and procedure. That is enough for one session.

If they return, having decided without any persuasion on my part that they desire the ministry of inner healing, then I take about ten minutes and again review the

Biblical, theological and psychological basis for inner healing.

Then I explain that people experience the revelation of Jesus through inner-healing in two primary ways. There are two primary ways people process information and two primary ways people remember the past.

One way is through prose. That is they think in words. When asked to remember an experience they remember it in words.

The other way is in pictures. They think in pictures. When they remember an experience they have a picture of it in their mind.

Primary is a key word. We are not locked into one way or another any more than an introvert or extrovert is locked into a behavior, but there is usually a primary way we function.

For example, when asked to remember a classroom, a person who thinks in words will have descriptive words come to mind; like the teachers desk, the color, their desk, other students etc. A person who thinks in pictures will see the classroom in their memory.

This is important because many times when ministering inner-healing people will experience it in the primary way they process information, i.e. through words or pictures.

If a person remembers in words then they may not see a memory, but will have word descriptions. When the Holy Spirit reveals the presence of Christ they may not see anything but will be aware of His presence. The communication will be in words rather than pictures.

Chapter Six: Ministering Inner Healing

It is helpful to ask a person how they process information. If a person thinks in words then they may not have pictures in their mind but they may have word impressions. If this happens then work with it and don't wait for pictures.

Sometimes a person begins with an awareness of His presence and the communication begins in words and then there are pictures.

If there are word impressions ask what they are. If he is not sure if the impressions are from the Holy Spirit or their own thoughts have them ask. If they receive the impression that the words are from the Holy Spirit ask them if they can accept that. If they still wonder have them tell the Lord that and have them ask the Lord for help.

The object is for them to gain confidence that they are hearing the Lord and it is not their own thoughts. You must not suggest it is the Lord, they need to come to that conclusion. You can help them by suggesting questions they can ask. You may also ask them if the thoughts are natural to their way of thinking. If it is not then they can conclude they are hearing words that are not their own.

Whether they see pictures or sense words the process is the same

Now we are ready to begin.

First, we pray together thanking Christ for His love, mercy, and faithfulness. We thank Him for the Holy Spirit who dwells within us and ministers to us, and we affirm our trust in the Holy Spirit to be in control. Remember, if we ask for bread He will not give us a stone.

Next, I request the person to close their eyes and ask the Holy Spirit to bring any memory to mind that He chooses. I ask them as the memory comes to mind to describe it to me. Then I remain silent until they speak. If a long time lapses, I may ask if any memory is coming to mind.

A question often asked is, "How will I know if the memory that comes is from my own thoughts or if it is by the Holy Spirit?" The answer is: if we have asked the Holy Spirit to take control of what ever memory comes, we can believe He will. If a memory is coming from my own thoughts, it is a simple matter for the Holy Spirit to give me another memory. If He doesn't, then I can regard that the memory from my own thoughts is the same as the Holy Spirit would bring.

Sometimes the memory that comes to mind seems so insignificant that the individual hesitates to mention it and waits for another. If that is the case, then I remind them that the Holy Spirit knows their need. Many times it is the seemingly insignificant experiences that became building blocks for wrong attitudes and behavior patterns.

Sometimes the memory is so painful they don't want to deal with it. Don't force them. Let it go. They may want to deal with it later. At times they hesitate to share the memory because of the nature of the event, such as committing adultery, abusing a child, or being abused as a child. Again, don't force the issue. People need the freedom to choose whether or not to reveal their memories. The Lord gives each of us free choice, and we need to honor that. We should give people freedom without applying pressure. By pressure, I mean making statements such as, "You will never be healed if you don't

Chapter Six: Ministering Inner Healing

deal with it now," or, "You have come this far, don't stop now."

I have found that, if an individual has gone through the pain of sharing the essence of their problem, when they return they are ready to deal with whatever memory comes. When they hesitate to share a particularly painful memory, the counselor who responds by not pressuring, will find they will eventually deal with it.

What does the counselor do when the counselee asks the Holy Spirit to bring whatever needs to be remembered and nothing happens. The person draws a blank.

This may be an indication of a mental block caused by anxiety indicating a fear of the process. Sometimes there is a fear that they will fail in the process. Sometimes there is a fear that there is some monster lurking in the subconscious. Most of the time when the monster is revealed it is a mouse with a microphone.

On occasion drawing a blank is an indication that there is not a need for inner-healing. As I wrote earlier I disagree with the notion that every person needs inner-healing, or that inner-healing is the only effective model of counseling. Size eight shoes are great if there is a person with size eight feet. Not everyone has the same needs and not every person responds to a particular model the same way.

When a person draws a blank for whatever reason, a way to get started is to ask the person to remember one of the happiest times in their life. Have them describe it to you in detail. Then ask them to close their eyes and remember that event. When they have it focused in their memory then ask the Holy Spirit to reveal the presence of Christ in that event.

The reason this approach may work is that the Holy Spirit is revealing Christ's presence in a non- threatening event. When they become aware of His presence they you can guide them in prayer by asking questions like:

What is Christ's attitude? For example, is He happy, sad, etc. How does He see you? Can you except that?

Does He love you? Can you accept that? If not tell Him and ask Him how that makes Him feel. Can you tell Him you are sorry and ask His forgiveness, etc. Is there anything else He wants to reveal to from this memory?

Is there any other memory where He wants to take you?

Note: If at any time there is a negative response to a question, such as, "does He love you?" and they say "no" or "I don't know", or He says "yes" but they have a hard time thinking it is Him speaking follow it up with a question. Questions like: Ask Him why? Ask Him if it is Him speaking? Ask Him how your doubt makes Him feel, ask Him if He will help you to believe? etc. Never suggest the answer, they need to hear the answer from Him in their spirit.

Usually one memory is all that should be dealt with at a time. There needs to be time to process the information. The exception would be when they are beginning with a memory of a good experience.

End the memory part of the session with the question, "Is there another memory or place He wants to take you. Go there. Then when that memory is in focus you can begin the next session with that memory.

After the memory session say, "let's talk about it". Review what the Lord told them in the memory, the areas

Chapter Six: Ministering Inner Healing

that were healed etc. Their articulating the experience in the memory helps to confirm it.

As they describe the memory, I ask questions regarding the details of the memory. For example, if they are in a kitchen, I may ask if they can see furniture, like the table, etc., or if they can see the floor covering. I will then ask if they can see the other people clearly. If there is conversation, I ask if they can hear it clearly. You do this in order to lock in on the memory, to bring the memory into clear focus. If it is a memory of a sordid affair, you don't need to ask questions about details as long as it is evident that the memory is vivid.

If the memory is not clear, or if it seems to come and go, then I leave it alone. If a memory is being brought to mind by the Holy Spirit, it will be clear. We don't have to force memory. If a person is being asked to remember a trauma, it will be a matter of them describing what they have been trying to forget.

If the memory is from very early childhood, it may take a while for it to come into focus. As you ask questions regarding the memory it will become more vivid.

When the memory is locked in, the person will experience the emotions associated with the memory. They will experience the fear, anxiety, anger, guilt or whatever emotions were present in the experience. It is helpful if you keep your eyes open so you can watch the countenance of the person. You will often be able to see the emotional response.

When they are experiencing the emotions of the memory, it is time to ask the Holy Spirit to reveal Christ in the situation. Simply say, "Christ is there with you. You may not have known Him yet, or have been aware of

His presence, but He is there. We are now going to ask the Holy Spirit to reveal Christ's presence."

Then offer a simple prayer, "Holy Spirit, we ask You to reveal Christ's Presence in this situation." After you have prayed this prayer remain silent. After a time ask the person if they sense His presence. Remember "how" they sense His presence is not important. They may sense a light, a form, or just the reality of His presence. If they receive nothing, simply ask the Holy Spirit to reveal why. When they say "Yes," ask if they can locate the physical location of His presence.

Second, ask if they can sense His countenance. Is He sad, angry, understanding? Ask if Christ is communicating anything. DO NOT PUT WORDS IN CHRIST'S MOUTH, such as, "My child, you know I love you." You are to just ask questions.

You may want them to ask Christ to reveal to them the situation as He sees it. If appropriate, you may want them to ask Christ to reveal to them how He sees the other people that are involved in the memory. Also remember the person is now living in that memory, and seeing Christ in that situation. Your questions will be guided by the Holy Spirit and the situation.

The key issues that need to be dealt with are: receiving Christ's perspective of the situation, receiving Christ's perspective of the people involved, and the person seeing how their reaction caused the inner hurt. They need to be led to repentance, forgiveness, and forgiving those involved.

These issues may prompt questions like: Can you tell Christ you repent of your reaction? Will you ask Christ to forgive you? Will you tell Christ you forgive those involved?

Chapter Six: Ministering Inner Healing

You are only a facilitator. Once the memory is fixed and Christ's presence is known, let them commune with Christ with as little interference as possible. You may need to suggest some questions they could ask Christ, but if the communion with Christ is flowing, just sit back and enjoy His presence and ministry. There have been times when I have witnessed Christ minister to someone for forty-five minutes. It is a beautiful time of being with Him as He ministers to someone's need.

Again, let me emphasize that you are not in any way to manipulate the memory or attempt to change the situation. You are not to suggest where Christ may be or what He might be doing or saying. If you believe the person needs to be closer to Christ, simply ask them to ask Christ if He will come closer. I have had people ask Christ if He would hold them. Never tell them what you think Christ is going to do.

Always put it in the form of a question. I have had people ask Christ to hold them and He has responded by telling them to come to Him, or to forgive someone, etc.

After it becomes apparent that the memory has run its course then say, "Let us talk about it." In the discussion you simply review what has taken place. If this is the first time for a person to experience anything like this, I may ask if they were surprised to sense Christ's presence.

I often ask if He appeared where they expected Him to appear and if He said and did what they might have anticipated. Many times their answer is "No." This allows me to point out that this is evidence that the Holy Spirit revealed Him, and it was not a product of their visualization or imagination.

In fact, if they see Christ in an entirely predictable way and place, and especially if He is simply giving them Scriptural promises, and that in King James English, I suspect they are faking it.

If they say Christ's answer to a question is for example, "He told me to trust Him," I tell them to ask Christ what that means. Keep asking questions until the answers are specific. For example, trusting Him may mean reaching out to a husband, or backing away from a co-dependent relationship.

In our discussion, I simply affirm what they experienced with Christ. I may ask them, "Do you now know that you have forgiven that person?" "Do you have the assurance that Christ has forgiven you?" "Do you understand how your reaction caused the hurt?" "Do you have a better understanding of the root cause of your anger, resentment, etc.?"

Sometimes they need to take some action, such as telling a person that they forgive them, or telling a parent or spouse that they love them. If the person involved in the memory is deceased, then assure them that their conversation with Christ is sufficient. It is in His hands.

Going through one memory in a session is sufficient ministry for anyone to receive at one time. They need time to assimilate the experience and recover from all the emotional reactions they have just had. So I set another time for us to get together.

You know the healing is complete when no more memories surface. I reject the idea that a person needs to systematically go through their whole life back to birth or conception. I do not believe it is necessary to ask someone to try to recall each year or time period of their life.

The Holy Spirit knows the key situations of our life that need healing, and we can trust Him to be faithful to search us out. We can pray with David in confidence,

> *Search me, O God, and know my heart; Try me and know my anxious thoughts; And see if there be any hurtful way in me, And lead me in the everlasting way.*
>
> (Psalm 139:23-24)

Again, I caution that not everyone is a candidate for inner healing. I only minister inner healing when there is recurring sin, such as a compulsive behavior that hasn't yielded to repentance and discipline.

An important observation and understanding is that after a person has been set free from a compulsion that has caused a behavior or attitude problem, it does not automatically follow that the behavior will immediately cease. Now the person has to break the habit that has been formed.

If a person has been a compulsive liar, after the compulsion has been healed, the habit of lying will remain and needs to be broken. The good news is that habits are quickly and easily broken if they are not driven by a compulsion.

For example, if you get a new keyboard that has the extracurricular keys in a different place it will be difficult for a few days. But it will surprise you in how short a time you will form new typing habits to fit the new keyboard.

When a person is highly motivated for change and the inner drive has been healed, the change comes rather quickly, but it is not automatic.

Another question that arises is, "Can a person minister inner healing to themselves?" My experience with people has been that after they have gone through several sessions and had strong experiences of Christ's presence being in a memory and ministering to them, some have been able to experience this in their own prayer time.

My suggestion would be that if you believe you need inner healing and your attempt at self ministry is unsuccessful, find someone who ministers inner healing. When you are seeking someone who ministers inner healing, ask if they practice visualization. If they do, I would not become involved.

One final word. As a person goes back in memory, the Holy Spirit may take them back to a childhood period and reveal experiences that happened to them before they could remember anything. On some rare occasions people have been taken back between conception and birth. Don't worry about that. If the Holy Spirit brings that to mind, when He reveals Christ's presence, He will minister to them in that situation. Many times, I have witnessed people being taken back to an age before memory can be recalled. When they had opportunity to check it out with parents, etc., they discovered the memory was accurate.

Some wonder whether the people are in a hypnotic state during the memory. Even though the Holy Spirit may be bringing something to mind that is before they were old enough to remember, they are not in a hypnotic state. A hypnotic state may seem similar, but I believe this is a valid ministry of the Holy Spirit bringing something to mind and not hypnosis.

CHAPTER SEVEN

Some Case Histories

For obvious reasons the names and places have been changed to protect those involved. These case histories are taken from over a fifteen–year period and involve counseling both as a pastor and in traveling ministry. Because I was a pastor in the same community for eighteen years, I have not used any case histories of people who were part of my church fellowship, except one which I will identify. In some situations, I have changed the circumstances involved so the persons concerned could not be recognized. The events and results of the ministry are as they happened.

Jim and Jane came to me seeking help after I had given a lecture on the subject of inner healing at a special meeting. They were in their late forties, had several grown children, and had been active in Christian work for a number of years. Jane was suffering from severe anxiety attacks. She had a very poor self image and was not able to receive love and affirmation of her worth or work.

She was a very giving person and was loved and appreciated by her husband, children, and those who knew her. Yet she really didn't believe anyone could love her for who she was. She had a good solid Biblical background and knew that she was saved, because she placed her confidence in the Word of God. Yet deep down, she wondered how Jesus could really love her.

She spent a lot of her life serving people, but for the wrong reason. She needed their approval. No matter how much she did or how much she gave, inwardly she felt it wasn't enough. Her husband loved her, but no matter how many times he told her, or what he did to show it, she doubted it.

You can imagine how this frustrated both of them. They were a lovely couple, yet she was driven by a need to feel accepted and loved.

Much of the ministry they had received to deal with Jane's problem centered around exhortations to place trust in Christ's love, and to have confidence in the Word of God. She accepted the fact that Christ died for her, but it made her feel so guilty, for how could He love her? She knew what she was supposed to believe, but that didn't alter the fact of her deep inner feelings. The more she was told that the answer was for her to trust, the more guilty she felt.

Having known her and a little of her life, it was hard for me to realize that she couldn't accept the fact that she was loved, for she was such a likable person. But the problem was she had to do things to be liked; yet no matter how many friends she had or how much people showed their appreciation, inwardly she was not able to receive it. In fact, it made her feel more guilty. She felt like a hypocrite.

As we talked she shared that she had some insight into her problem. Her mother had rejected her from birth. Her mother had not hidden that she was an unwanted child,

Chapter Seven: Some Case Histories

and that she was in the way. Her mother had often told her that she was not wanted and called her stupid, etc.

To her knowledge, she had forgiven her mother and did not harbor resentment. Yet she couldn't find victory over her inner feelings that were contrary to what she believed. She believed that Christ loved her and had received her as His child. She believed her husband loved her; she believed her children loved her; but this very belief haunted her with feelings of condemnation because of her poor self image.

Even though they had heard an extensive lecture on the subject of inner healing, I took time to explain that in Christ there was no past, only the present. I explained that the Holy Spirit could be trusted to bring to her memory anything that needed to be healed, and as she remembered, she could trust the Holy Spirit to reveal Christ. I took time to discuss the difference between revelation by the Holy Spirit of Christ and her trying to visualize Christ.

She closed her eyes in prayer and asked the Holy Spirit to take control of her mind and thoughts and to bring anything to memory that needed to be healed.

In a few moments I asked her if anything was coming to her memory. She said yes, that she was in a crib crying and her mother had come in to make her be quiet. I asked, "How old are you?" She said around 18 months. All of a sudden she began to cry and shake and cry, "No, No." I asked her what was happening. She said her mother was holding a pillow over her face trying to suffocate her. I asked if she could see the pillow. She said she could before her mother put it over her face; she said she could hear her mother screaming at her.

I asked the Holy Spirit to reveal Christ. She saw a light enter the room and it was between her and her mother. Then she saw a hand take her mother's arm and pull the pillow away. She said the hand was Jesus' hand. Then she grew calm and for a long time just rocked back and forth. Her husband and I watched this for over twenty minutes. I asked her what was happening, and she said Christ was holding her and telling her He had protected her and that He loved her.

I asked her to ask Christ to reveal her mother to her as He saw her. She began to weep. She said she saw her mother's frustration, anger, hurt and fear. I asked her if she could tell Jesus that she forgave her mother. She did.

I asked her if she could confess to Jesus how hard it had been for her to trust His love. She confessed that and broke into tears of confession and repentance. She said that Jesus assured her that she was forgiven.

Because we were at a special session out of town and I would not see her again, we did continue to pray. Another memory came to her. She remembered being in the water and being drawn under by a strong current. I asked her how old she was, and she said around eight. I asked if she could feel the water around her; she said, "Yes," and began to shake. We asked the Holy Spirit to reveal Christ's presence. She didn't see anything, but felt His presence as she was brought to shore and saved from drowning.

She said she knew Christ was with her and it was because of Him that her life was saved. (She wrote to me later stating that she had not been bothered with a fear of rejection since that session.)

After this experience, we discussed her experiences

for a while. I asked her what she thought she should do concerning the revelation she had received about her mother. She said she wanted to let her know that she had forgiven her and that she loved her.

Several months later, I received a letter from Jim and Jane. They wrote that they had visited her mother and felt led to share that she knew that her mother had almost smothered her with a pillow when she was an infant, and she described the pillow. The mother turned pale and asked how she knew that. The mother said that no one knew, that she had shared it with no one, not even her husband. When Jane explained how the Holy Spirit had revealed it to her, that she understood the anguish her mother was experiencing, that it was Christ who pulled her hand away, and that she had forgiven her, they wept together. The mother was able to accept Christ's forgiveness, and mother and daughter were united in love.

Most importantly, Jim wrote that Jane was able to receive love and affirmation from her family and friends. She was set free from her anxiety attacks and was able to give out of an overflowing love rather than a drive to be accepted.

George came to me with a problem of bisexuality. He was married and had a young daughter. He loved his wife and daughter, but his homosexual temptations were keeping him in guilt and defeat. He had hoped that when he became a Christian, his problem would be solved. He had had some Bible School training, and had been a Christian for over ten years. He had tried everything he knew and still was haunted by these homosexual temptations.

He came to me because he, like Jim and Jane, had attended a seminar that I led on the subject of inner healing. After he shared his problem and I went over the Biblical and theological foundations of inner healing, and explained the process, we were ready to begin.

We prayed and waited for the Holy Spirit to bring a memory to mind. He began to describe a situation when he was about eight years old. He and a cousin were exposing themselves to each other in an upstairs bedroom when an older cousin walked in on them and asked them what they were doing.

I asked him whether he could see the room clearly, and if he could hear his cousin clearly'? He said he could, and it was obvious that he was very embarrassed and ashamed.

We asked the Holy Spirit to reveal Christ's presence. He was hesitant, for he was ashamed to see Christ in that situation. But after waiting a while, he asked the Holy Spirit to reveal Christ. He saw Christ's presence standing between him and his older cousin. He said Christ was grieved and weeping. I asked him if he knew why Christ was weeping. He said that Christ was weeping because he was so ashamed. Christ told George that he didn't need to be ashamed, that he was just learning about sexuality and what it was to be a boy. Christ told him that his older cousin wouldn't think of this incident much after this day.

George confessed his behavior and shame to Christ, and Christ assured him that he was forgiven. Christ went on to tell George that He made him a man, and that it was all right to be a man. He told George that he didn't need to be ashamed of being a man.

After this I said, "Let's discuss it for a moment." We discussed the fact that George knew that he was forgiven. He explained the tremendous feeling he had about being a man. Without fully realizing it, George was ashamed of being a man because of this experience. Apparently, this shame caused him to reject his sexuality, and it expressed itself in homosexual feelings.

I don't pretend to understand all of the psychological dynamics of this experience. I do know that in traditional counseling I wouldn't have told George that their sexual behavior as a child was all right. I may have explained that it was normal behavior for two eight-year-old boys, but I surely would not have indicated that in Christ's eyes it was O.K. Nor should we conclude that this would be Christ's response for every such experience. Only He knows the real motives of the heart.

After this one experience George was set free of his homosexual temptations. His relationship with his wife obviously improved. He was able to make love with her without guilt.

I would like to mention that I have refrained from sharing these experiences for years, feeling that folk would reject these dramatic healings as a quick fix. For a long time, I questioned them myself. I have witnessed people being set free in one to several sessions that traditional counseling would take years to accomplish, if it was accomplished at all.

Note that in both of the above cases I did not make a second appointment to minister inner healing as I have suggested in the previous chapter. The reason is that they had attended a session on inner healing and that is the reason they came. If they had come to me for counseling without receiving prior information about inner healing, I would have explained it and given them time to make a decision regarding the process.

Mike had attended a seminar on inner healing that I had conducted for Christian counselors. In fact Mike's theological background had caused him to reject the idea that the gifts of the Spirit were for today. He believed that they were for the Apostles and the birth of the Church and had ceased with the death of the Apostles. Yet he felt that there might be something to this inner healing.

He had battled a problem of gluttony ever since he had been a Christian. He was at least 100 pounds over weight. He knew it hurt his witness and counseling ministry. He had dieted, fasted, prayed and exercised all the will power he could muster, and everything had ended in miserable failure. He lived with guilt, condemnation, and of course a terrible self image. One problem with the sin of gluttony is that people "wear" it. It is seldom a hidden sin.

After a review of the basis and process of inner healing, Mike asked the Holy Spirit to bring anything to mind that needed to be healed. After a while, a scene came to mind from when he was about six years old. He had been visiting his grandmother. He spent a lot of time with his grandmother, and he loved her very much. Her reputation for being a good cook was known far and wide.

In this memory, his grandmother had made Mike's favorite pie and some of his favorite cookies. Even though Mike was full, his grandmother urged Mike to eat more. Mike remembered feeling full, but was also afraid of hurting his grandmothers feelings if he didn't force himself to eat more. I asked him if he could see the kitchen clearly, and if he could hear his grandmother's voice clearly. When he said he could, we asked the Holy Spirit to reveal Christ's presence.

Mike felt Christ's presence standing by him. Christ

was grieved. I instructed Mike to ask Christ why He was grieved, and Christ responded that He was grieved because his grandmother's misapplied love was hurting Mike. He told Mike that he was receiving the impression within his inner thoughts that the way to please people he loved, and to be considered a good boy was to overeat. Eating what was prepared was a way for him to express his love for the person who prepared the food.

I asked Mike to ask Christ to reveal how He saw his grandmother. Christ revealed to Mike that his grandmother received her self worth from being a good cook. When people indulged in her cooking, she was affirmed as a person. She had no intention of hurting anyone, but Mike was receiving an inner attitude that would lead to gluttony.

I asked Mike to confess his over eating as a sin and ask for Christ's forgiveness. He did and Christ assured him he was forgiven. I asked him to tell Christ that he forgave his grandmother. He did. I then asked him to request that Christ reveal to him how He saw Mike. Christ revealed that He had been patient with Mike regarding his gluttony for He understood its cause: and He was grieved at the pain it was causing him. He assured Mike that overeating was not an appropriate way to express love and appreciation.

After Mike communicated with Christ for awhile, I suggested we talk about it. During that conversation we discussed Mike's insights. I reaffirmed with him Christ's love and forgiveness. Then I explained that Christ had healed Mike's compulsion to overeat. Now he had to exercise discipline and break the overeating habit.

I suggested that he eliminate sugar from his diet, for that activates the insulin and increases the appetite. I also suggested he not go on a diet, but gradually change his eating habits so that he would begin losing about a pound per week.

I affirmed to him that this time he would be able to exercise discipline where he had failed before, because now the compulsive motivation had been removed. After several more sessions, scheduled two to three weeks apart to monitor Mike's progress and encourage him in his new life style, it was apparent that he felt much better about himself, was losing weight, and was not craving food.

A young lady we will call Barbara came to me in desperation. She had been a Christian for a number of years, and was an active leader in her local church. Several years before, she had been beaten and raped on a cold winter night in a major city. She was attacked as she walked to her automobile in a dark parking area.

She came to me because she knew she needed to forgive the two young men who had done this, but all she could feel was anger, resentment, and hate. She was plagued with nightmares. The counsel she had received had been personally supportive, but her pastor pointed out that she could not get free of her feelings until she forgave the two men. She knew this, but no matter how hard she tried, she could not change her feelings.

She had told the Lord she was willing to be willing. She tried to let go of anger and hate. She was not interested in revenge, but wanted to be free from the effects of the experience.

She came to me saying something like, "I have tried everything. I know what I must do, but I can't. If you can't help me, I don't know what I will do. I realize if I don't forgive these men, Jesus won't forgive me. Please, can you help me?"

Chapter Seven: Some Case Histories

I knew that if she met Jesus in that situation she could be healed and set free. I took over an hour to explain the basis for inner healing, and the process of how it was ministered. I emphasized that she would have to remember what she had been trying to forget. She would have to deliberately remember that awful experience and describe it until it was vivid in her memory and emotions. I assured her that Christ would meet her there and minister to her.

After sharing on the ministry of inner healing and the risk and trauma of experiencing the violation again, I asked her to think about it for a few days and if she wanted to proceed to call me for an appointment.

In several days she called and we set a time to get together. At the second meeting I reviewed the basis and procedure for inner healing and asked if she had any questions.

We prayed together. I prayed that we were glad that we could trust the faithfulness of the Holy Spirit to guide her memory, and the love of Christ to give her strength to emotionally experience this trauma again, and we trusted that this time Christ would minister to Barbara in the situation so she could be set free.

She was hesitant and I did not press the issue, but she was so desperate that she was willing to suffer whatever she had to in order to be set free. As she began to remember her experience, it came to her in vivid detail. As she described it she quickly went into the same emotions of terror that she experienced that cold winter night.

As she became hysterical, I asked the Holy Spirit to reveal Christ's presence. Immediately she saw the light of His presence.

I have to admit that many times in these situations I tend to be judgmental. If Christ is there why doesn't He protect His child? If I were going through such a terrible experience and I saw Christ standing there watching, I would want to ask Him why He didn't do something. I would feel like the Apostles who were in the boat that was being swamped by a storm while Christ was asleep on a pillow in the back. The Apostles cried out, "*Master, don't you care that we perish?*" I have been amazed that although these were my thoughts, never once has a person who has seen Christ in these types of situations ever been judgmental of Christ. I haven't shared my feelings with them. I am grateful for His mercy toward me for having these thoughts.

When she saw Christ's presence she calmed down a bit. I asked her to ask Christ to reveal to her how He saw these two young men. She did, and her hysteria turned to a wailing. I asked her what was happening, and she said she saw the darkness of their souls. She also saw that they were on drugs. She felt Christ's grieving spirit for them.

I asked her if she could tell Jesus that she forgave them for what they were doing. Would you believe, it was easy for her. She did more than just ask Christ to forgive them; she plead for His mercy on them, and prayed that they would come to know Him as their loving Lord and Savior. It reminded me of Stephen's prayer as he was being stoned to death. Heaven opened and he saw Christ and cried out for mercy on them.

Then she became quiet and I asked her what was happening. She said that the men had fled and she was there in the cold with her clothes mostly ripped off. I asked her if Christ was still there and she said, "Yes." I

Chapter Seven: Some Case Histories

asked her if she would ask Christ to show her how He saw her. She began to weep gentle tears. She said, "He is telling me that in His eyes I am pure." I asked her to ask Christ if He would hold her. It became evident as I watched her that He did. I then suggested that she tell Christ she was sorry for the anger, hate, resentment, and fear that she had within. He said He forgave her and that it was already gone.

I then suggested we discuss it. In our discussion I asked her if she really expected to see Christ. She said, "No, it was a surprise." She said she was amazed that when she saw Him, even in the midst of the rape, that she felt no shame in the presence of His holiness. She felt his love and compassion. She remarked that that was how the woman caught in adultery must have felt. I asked her if she believed she had forgiven the young men. She said, "Yes, I have no doubt about it." I asked her if she knew she was forgiven. She said "Yes." If you could have seen the relief on her face, you would have known she had been set free.

In subsequent sessions there were some more inner healing experiences from her childhood. But it is important to note that from that first session she had no more nightmares regarding that experience. She was free and she knew His love in a deeper dimension.

I need to comment that I am glad I had been through inner healing ministry many times before this dramatic case. Even at that, in the midst of these emotions, I had flashes of doubt. Suppose the person becomes hysterical and the Holy Spirit doesn't reveal Christ? HE HAS ALWAYS BEEN FAITHFUL.

The only times there has been no revelation of Christ by the Holy Spirit are when the person later admitted that they had made up the story of the memory to test me. All sorts of weird things happen in the counseling room. Also, I have had people say they didn't want to see Christ in a particular situation. They could confess it to me, but seeing Christ in the situation was more than they were willing to handle. This has happened several times when a person has confessed to being unfaithful in their marriage and they didn't want to see Christ in that situation.

I am going to share two more cases. One we will call Sue. Sue's pastor asked me if I would meet with her. I had shared some of the principles of inner healing with the pastor, and he said he had been meeting with a member of his congregation and he felt she needed inner healing. He talked with Sue and she agreed to see me.

Her problem was that even though she had a good husband and family, and a good job, she always acted to destroy good things that were happening to her. For example, she had had several good jobs and when the big promotion was about to come, she would do something to torpedo the promotion. She would say or do inappropriate things such as staying home from work or not meeting deadlines that she easily could have met.

When things were going very well at home, she would become irritable and be nasty to her husband. She would do this until there was a blow-up, then they would start over. She wondered how many more of these cycles he could go through. One final thing was that she was a chain smoker, and she had a suspicion that it was caused more from a hidden death wish than addiction to nicotine.

I explained the basis and process of inner healing and gave her time to think about it. When we came back together we reviewed inner healing and prayed asking the Holy Spirit to bring anything to memory that needed healing. After a time of silence I asked her if she was remembering anything. She said that she was in a one room school and the teacher was punishing her for giving a flippant answer to a question. She said that the teacher made her stand in a trash can with a dunce cap on and the other students were laughing and making fun of her.

She could see the teacher very clearly, even the dress she was wearing. She could hear the students laughing and some of the remarks they were making. She felt her shame and her anger toward the teacher.

We asked the Holy Spirit to reveal Christ. She saw the light of His presence in the front of the class room between her and the students. I asked her to ask Christ to reveal to her how He saw that teacher. She began to describe the teacher's frustration and anger. She also saw the teacher's fear of failure. She saw that teacher as an emotionally needy person who felt alone and over her head with the class, especially with Sue, who was a very bright child. She saw that the teacher actually believed that this young child was smarter than she was. This was an amazing revelation to Sue.

I asked Sue if she could tell Jesus that she forgave the teacher for what she did. She was able to do that. Then I asked her if she would tell Jesus that she was sorry for the anger, resentment, and hate she felt toward the teacher and the students. She did, and said that Christ told her she was forgiven.

I asked her to ask Christ to reveal how He saw her. She began to describe herself as a bright, loving child whom Christ loved. She also saw her sin of pride mixed with fear. But Christ told her that when she accepted Him as Lord and Savior she was forgiven of that and He had made her a new creation.

Jesus also told her that as His child, she was loved, and she deserved what He was giving her. She deserved it because she was His child and He loved her, not because she earned it. Christ asked her if she would accept His love and that He was making it possible for her to receive these good things. She responded, "Yes."

I asked her where she was at present, and she said that she was still in the trash can. I asked her to ask Christ if He would take her out of the trash can. She said that it became clear to her that when the teacher allowed her to take the dunce cap off and step out of the trash can, Christ was there. He revealed to her that she did not belong in a trash can.

As we discussed this experience, we went over her relief at forgiving the teacher and the other students. She said she felt whole inside for the first time in her life.

I did remind her that she would have to break these destructive thought patterns. That would not be automatic, but it would be possible because their underlying causes had been healed.

I learned later that she had quit smoking, accepted a good promotion, and things were very good at home. It became evident in this situation, that Sue felt unworthy of love or success, and when they came her way she would do things to sabotage them.

I mentioned earlier that one of the cases that would be shared would not be an assumed name. I have left it until last. I cannot use an assumed name because the

Chapter Seven: Some Case Histories

situation was so unusual and well-publicized in the media that there was no way it could be disguised. I did ask permission to share the story.

Our son, James, has had a lot of surgery, and as a result he suffered a blood clot that caused him to black out while driving his car. The accident happened a couple of miles from his home and within a 1/2 mile of his destination. As he approached a stop sign that was at a canal bridge, he blacked out and drove into the canal. His car turned over, end for end, settling upside down in the water.

At the other four-way stop sign was a paramedic, and running on a bike path along the canal was an off duty police officer. Both of them jumped into the water, and after several dives, realized that the car was a four door and was upside down. By this time a number of people were in the water, and they turned the car right side up and freed him. All of this took about eight to ten minutes. It is estimated that Jim was under water at least five to eight minutes.

The accident received much publicity because it was so unusual. Also, I was chaplain of the fire department that answered the rescue call and didn't know who was involved until we arrived on the scene. Because of these circumstances it was in the major newspapers and on TV. It was such a dramatic story that a week later it was reviewed as part of the stories of the week.

Both James and his wife realized that had a paramedic and police officer not been at the scene, the probability of Jim's survival was nil We all realize that the right people being at the right place at the right time saved Jim's life.

Even so, knowing that and having an inner assurance of Christ's love are two different matters. Of course, I have to admit that my question was, "Lord, why didn't you prevent the blackout for at least another five minutes, when Jim would have been at his destination?" The Lord is gracious with us as we question Him. I praise God for his infinite love and patience with us.

Jim became conscious for a short time while he was trapped upside down in the car. He remembered trying to unfasten the seat belt, but his body weight against the buckle had it jammed. He remembered hearing the water rush in and feeling it on his body. Then he lost consciousness again until he was being put in the ambulance.

His problem was that he was having nightmares and flashbacks of this experience. When he shared this with me, we prayed together about it. Later, as I thought about it, it occurred to me that possibly Christ would heal this memory and set him free of the nightmares.

I shared with Jim the basis of inner healing and asked him to think about it. If he wanted me to, I would minister to him. After a while he asked me if I would. My wife and I met with him at his home. I again went over the basis of inner healing and the procedure we would follow.

As Jim described what he remembered of the accident, he began to shake. It was evident he was experiencing the emotions of the accident. We asked the Holy Spirit to reveal Christ's presence. Soon Jim became calm. I asked him if he was aware of Christ's presence. He said that he felt His presence between him and the windshield of the car.

Chapter Seven: Some Case Histories

Jim then said that Christ was assuring him that He is Lord and that He is in control of Jim's life and this situation. Then a strange thing happened. Jim went limp, as if he were asleep. He remained that way for a period of time. I asked him what was happening. He said that he was still in the car and he was unconscious, but Christ was still there and telling him, even though he was unconscious and helpless, that He is Lord and in control of the situation.

I asked Jim if he would confess his faith in Christ as Lord of his life, and thank Him for being in control. Then I suggested that Jim confess his fear, etc., as sin and ask for Christ's forgiveness. He did that and said that he knew Christ forgave him.

In the discussion that followed, I asked Jim if he had an assurance of Christ's love and Lordship over his life. He said that he did. I also pointed out that at the time of the experience he wasn't responsible for his fear and lack of faith, but when he saw it in his memory and was aware of Christ's presence then he became responsible for these things.

This experience happened over a year before the time of this writing and Jim, to this time, has not had another flashback or nightmare.

I have shared these case histories with the hope that it will encourage those who need inner healing and also as a teaching tool of the concepts that are found in the preceding chapters.